I0813998

THE STORY OF
Ferrari

First published in 2021 by Welbeck
An imprint of Headline Publishing Group Limited

7

Cataloguing in Publication Data is available from the British Library

ISBN 978 1 78739 924 2

Printed and bound in Italy

Headline's policy is to use papers that are natural, renewable and recyclable products and made from wood grown in well-managed forests and other controlled sources. The logging and manufacturing processes are expected to conform to the environmental regulations of the country of origin.

Editor: Ross Hamilton
Design: Eliana Holder & Luana Gobbo
Picture Research: Paul Langan
Production: Arlene Alexander

HEADLINE PUBLISHING GROUP LIMITED
A Hachette UK Company
Carmelite House
50 Victoria Embankment
London EC4Y 0DZ

The authorised representative in the EEA is Hachette Ireland,
8 Castlecourt Centre, Dublin 15, D15 XTP3, Ireland (email: info@hbgi.ie)

www.headline.co.uk
www.hachette.co.uk

A TRIBUTE TO AUTOMOTIVE EXCELLENCE

STUART CODLING

Ferrari

CONTENTS

BIRTH OF A LEGEND

BUILDING THE DREAM

Il Commendatore. Il Drake. L'Ingegnere ("the Commander", "the Drake", "the Engineer"), "Agitator of men." Enzo Anselmo Ferrari gratefully assumed many titles, ranging from grandiose to enigmatic, over the course of a long and eventful life. Fittingly, perhaps, the myths surrounding that life even shroud the date his given name was inked into the records: Ferrari's own official origin story has it that Enzo was born in Modena on 18 February 1898 but, owing to a blizzard, this fact wasn't registered with the authorities until two days later.

Then as now, compliance with such niceties as official paperwork was a low priority for the average citizen of what was a young kingdom, unified within the lifetime of Enzo's parents, Alfredo and Adalgisa. Turmoil continued to be a fact of life in a nation which had once been home to one of Europe's defining civilisations and then, after that empire's fall, become a seething hotbed of rival city states defined by great artworks and rampant infighting, frequently invaded by neighbouring dynasties. Nationalism fuelled the movement towards unification and, by the end of the 19th century,

OPPOSITE: The young Enzo Ferrari dreamed of being an opera singer, journalist, or a racing driver

rapid industrialisation in the north of Italy would make the country one of Europe's powers – without fully addressing the inequalities which would fuel ongoing social fractures in the century to come.

It was a world of chaos and poverty, but also of great opportunities for the likes of Enzo Ferrari, ambitious men who learned very quickly how to make the right connections. Above all, Enzo Ferrari was a different man to different people, an empire-builder who came to relish his role as the spider in the centre of an elaborate tangle of intrigues.

During the glory days of the Roman Empire, the Emilia-Romagna region was colonised by former legionaries who were granted parcels of land upon completing 25 years' service to the empire. Modena was one of many settlements which grew up along the *Via Aemilia*, the Roman road connecting Piacenza to Rimini. Enzo's mother hailed from Forli, the walled city on the other side of Bologna snatched by the Borgias in the 15th century. Enzo's father's trade was one which had not only survived, but thrived in the transition to industry: metalwork. Modena rang to the sound of hammers in the many workshops around the town, manufacturing such items as once formed the underpinnings of carts and which now clothed and sprung the motor car. In time this area would become a hub of artisan design and coachbuilding for the automobile industry.

Enzo's father ran such a workshop, facilitating the family with the trappings of the middle class. In his autobiography *My Terrible Joys*, Enzo wrote of sharing a bedroom over the workshop with his older brother, Alfredo Jr, and being woken each morning by the ringing of hammers below. He took note of his father's organisational fastidiousness, acting as company secretary as well as the manager, designer and salesman.

Unlike his brother, Enzo was an indifferent and unmotivated scholar, frequently beaten by his father upon

ABOVE: Enzo Ferrari's driving talent and gift for making connections enabled him to secure a job with Alfa Romeo.

receipt of critical school reports. Enzo would never become the engineer his father desired him to be, though he willingly adopted the honorific title *L'Ingegnere*, He would, in time, become something rather greater, but his father did not live to see it. Alfredo Sr died of pneumonia in 1916, shortly after Enzo's 18th birthday. Alfredo Jr was away, having enlisted in the air force, and before the year was out he too was dead, of an illness which went unrecorded.

Enzo had dreamed of becoming a racing driver ever since his father took him to watch the 1908 Coppa Florio road race in Bologna; and if not that, perhaps an opera singer, or a sports journalist – a handful of his football reports were published in the *Gazzetta dello Sport*. But those lofty ambitions seemed gone as, in his father's absence, the family business collapsed and Enzo was drafted into the army, where he was tasked with shoeing mules in an artillery regiment. His one lucky break was that he survived the deadly 1918 flu pandemic, though it left him severely debilitated.

Returning to civilian life after the armistice, Enzo faced the prospect of building a life without the traditional family support network. "I was back where I had started [in Modena]," he wrote in his autobiography. "No money, no experience, limited education. All I had was a passion to get somewhere."

Turned down for an engineering job with Fiat in Turin, Enzo nevertheless demonstrated his knack for making connections, living modestly and securing work with CMN, one of many engineering companies making the transition from putting together military-industrial machinery to assembling passenger cars. Enzo's job was to test-drive and deliver these cars, and it enabled him to revive his dream of becoming a racing driver.

BELOW: Tazio Nuvolari and his Scuderia Ferrari mechanics push his Alfa Romeo onto the grid for the 1935 French Grand Prix.

ABOVE: German teams were dominant in the 1930s, but in the 1935 German GP Tazio Nuvolari beat them resoundingly on home ground in his Ferrari-run Alfa Romeo.

This was to be a short but instructive phase of Enzo's life. Thrilled by initial tastes in the Parma–Poggio di Berceto hillclimb and the Targa Florio road race aboard a CMN, he acquired a more powerful car, an ageing Isotta Fraschini 4.5-litre beast, for his return to the hillclimb, finishing third overall. For his second crack at the Targa Florio he looked to Milan and Alfa Romeo, then Italy's pre-eminent manufacturer of racing cars, as well as more humble machinery. Here he would lay the foundations of his future empire.

Alfa Romeo took on Enzo as a driver and he energetically expanded his role as a salesman and networker, helping the company recruit engineering and driving talent from the ailing CMN, as well as raiding Fiat for promising personnel. Most notably he was instrumental in the poaching of leading racecar engineer Vittorio Jano when Alfa's P1 grand prix car proved underwhelming. The work proved lucrative enough for Enzo to establish an Alfa Romeo dealership in his home town while still racing occasionally.

ABOVE: Tazio Nuvolari is a blur in his Alfa Romeo, occupying first position at the Nürburgring in 1935 on the way to a memorable victory.

The turning point came in July 1924. Enzo had won minor races but was not considered good enough to rank among Alfa's stars. In the high-profile Coppa Acerbo road race he won in a second-string car after team-mate Giuseppe Campari, driving Jano's mighty new P2, stopped with a burst tyre. This was enough to persuade Alfa competitions manager Giorgio Rimini to field Enzo in a P2 at the forthcoming French Grand Prix. The car was too powerful and unpredictable even for one so determined as Enzo, who suffered a panic attack and beat a retreat back to Italy. He would race again, but not at this level.

Three years later, Alfa Romeo also withdrew from grand prix racing, providing Ferrari with the germ of an idea. He now enjoyed connections with wealthy customers who nurtured a passion for racing, and with talented mechanics who knew their way around a racing car. Enzo put together a deal to create his own racing company, Scuderia Ferrari, with seed capital from two wealthy customers, plus a buy-in from Alfa Romeo – who understood the marketing value of retaining an involvement with motor racing – and Pirelli. Enzo would run the cars and all his customers had to do was turn up on the day to race.

This arrangement proved so successful that Scuderia Ferrari survived Alfa Romeo's return to grand prix racing, and its nationalisation by Benito Mussolini's fascist government in the early 1930s. In 1932 Ferrari adopted the prancing horse motif although, as with so many elements of the Ferrari story, scepticism surrounds the official account that it was the personal emblem of a fighter ace who served in the same squadron as Enzo's older brother.

What *is* well-documented is that the 1930s grand prix racing scene was co-opted by Nazi Germany as a prestige project. Hitler's government ploughed resources into Mercedes and Auto Union's advanced racing cars and Mussolini felt under pressure to do the same. Having taken responsibility for running Alfa's works racing machines

BELOW: A packed crowd watches Louis Chiron (leading) in his Alfa Romeo Tipo-B P3 during the 1934 French Grand Prix. He would go on to win the race.

2
2

post-nationalisation, Ferrari was outgunned on the track despite the valiant efforts of some of the best drivers of that generation, including Tazio Nuvolari. While Jano fell out of favour as a result, and was obliged to leave, Enzo's solution to the money-no-object German speed machines was to build cars which would race in a different class, thereby avoiding the humiliation of direct competition.

That notion didn't cut it with the echelons above. As Enzo's proposed car took shape, drawn by Jano's assistant, Gioachino Colombo, the political wheels continued to grind. Alfa Romeo bought Scuderia Ferrari in 1938, rendering Enzo an employee, then brought in a new design team led by an outsider, Wilfredo Ricart, for whom Enzo quickly developed an outright loathing.

Scuderia Ferrari ceased to exist, becoming Alfa Corse, and Enzo walked away to form a new company, Auto Avio Costruzioni, agreeing with his old employers not to race in opposition to them for four years, but World War II meant this agreement went untested. Ferrari's business churned out machine tools and aircraft parts for the Italian government, a prime example of Enzo *realpolitik*: this area of Italy was a communist stronghold and Enzo was always hard but scrupulously fair with his employees – while serving a regime implacably opposed to communism.

When motor racing spluttered into life after World War II, Ferrari felt the urge to go racing again. He contacted Colombo, then serving a suspension while his membership of the fascist party was investigated.

OPPOSITE: Rudolf Caracciola's Mercedes-Benz W25B (right) leads Tazio Nuvolari's Alfa Romeo during the 1935 French grand prix. Mercedes benefited from a huge influx of funding from the Nazi government during the 1930s.

E LA MACCHINA?

556
548

THE CAR'S THE STAR

"[Enzo] Ferrari's expectation of performance exerted a strong force that radiated throughout the organisation, and the drivers were not exempt from it," wrote the 1961 world champion Phil Hill. "Rather than the race being a culmination of a team effort to win, there was a feeling instead as if you, the driver, had been reluctantly entrusted with this gem of a machine, this fruit of genius, and hopefully your natural dunderheadedness would not destroy it."

"When one of us did win I sensed a certain reluctance on Ferrari's part to share the laurels with the driver, to pat him on the back and thank him for a job well done. It was more like Ferrari felt the victory was doubly his – he had not only managed to build a car that was better than all the other cars, but a car that was also good enough to foil even his driver's natural destructiveness."

The key to the Ferrari legend, that x-factor which makes its road cars such objects of desire and seats in its race cars so coveted, is the presence of the creator etched into the DNA.

OPPOSITE: Enzo Ferrari poses with three of the four 290 MMs built specifically to win the 1956 Mille Miglia road race. Number 600 (front), driven to fourth place by Juan Manuel Fangio, fetched more than $25 million at auction in 2015.

ABOVE: Eugenio Castellotti, seen here in a Ferrari 555 in the 1955 Dutch GP, died while testing a Ferrari in 1957.

Enzo's personality, his hopes and dreams, inhabit every car which rolls out of the factory gates.

When he began building cars under the Ferrari name again in 1947 he had already fathered two children: Alfredo, fondly known as Dino, aspired to be an engineer but died young of muscular dystrophy; Piero was born to Enzo's mistress and went unacknowledged publicly during Laura Ferrari's lifetime. Hill believed this left a hole in Enzo's life which he filled with work. Hill wrote, too, that Enzo's cars "were so directly an extension of his own being, to admit fault in them was to admit fault in himself".

Once back in business under his own name, Ferrari had little interest in building road cars, save where it would subsidise his racing activities. This would change as the financial burdens of racing grew, but Enzo had already proved himself a master salesman as well as a successful entrepreneur. As the legend grew, so too did the line of supplicants hoping to buy a piece of it.

There are those who claim Enzo ceased to travel and attend motor races after Dino's death in 1956, but in truth his wanderlust had long since been quenched. Ferrari preferred life in his new workshops in Maranello, just down the road from Modena, where he established his new kingdom. There he would pull strings, stoke rivalries, divide and rule.

BELOW: Ferrari's son Alfredo, known to all as Dino, had muscular dystrophy and died young.

Thanks partly to this kind of internal competition, it didn't take long for Ferrari to supplant Alfa Romeo as Italy's premier exponent of racing and performance cars. Before Gioachino Colombo's suspension was lifted and he returned to Alfa, he designed a diminutive but readily expandable 1.5-litre V12 which would power Ferrari's first racing cars. Reworked over the years with larger displacements and more sophisticated valve-gear, it would also see service in Ferrari road cars until the late 1980s.

Colombo's presence at Maranello overlapped with that of Aurelio Lampredi, a former scooter and aircraft engine designer who had a different vision: a larger all-aluminium V12 which, unlike Colombo's engine, wouldn't need supercharging to be competitive in what was soon to become known as Formula 1.

ABOVE: The troubled 555 'Super Squalo' took one grand prix win in 1954 but was quickly set aside.

Ferrari's first race car, the 125S, took its name from the swept volume (in cubic centimetres) of a single cylinder in the Colombo V12 which powered it. On 11 May 1947, Franco Cortese raced the prototype for the first time at Piacenza,

LEFT: Ferrari won 14 of the 17 races in the world championship's Formula 2 era from 1952-53. Alberto Ascari was responsible for 11 of them.

ABOVE: British drivers Mike Hawthorn and Peter Collins (foreground, left and right) were among Ferrari's star drivers in the 1950s. Hawthorn was the world champion in 1958.

briefly taking the lead before his fuel pump failed. Cortese had sold machine tools for Ferrari's Auto Avio Costruzione and told him he was insane to give that up for motor racing. Now he changed his tune, winning two weeks later in Rome, on a street circuit around the ancient baths of Caracalla. Ferrari also received a visit from his old friend Luigi Chinetti, a double winner of the Le Mans 24 Hours now settled in America – a promised land, home to dozens of wealthy amateurs who, he claimed, would leap at the chance to race an exotic European car.

In a continent shattered by war and still facing shortages of raw materials, motor racing offered precious entertainment for the masses and an adrenaline buzz for a new wave of participants who had seen combat and struggled to adapt to

BELOW: Luigi Musso carried Ferrari's – and the nation's – hopes of being an Italian world champion, but he pushed too hard in the 1958 French GP and crashed fatally.

peacetime life. Most of the cars were pre-war stock which had survived being melted down for munitions.

Not that this meant Ferrari would have an easy ride. The ladder-frame chassis of the early cars were crude and flimsy, not that this mattered greatly to Enzo, who believed the engine to be the greatest performance differentiator (later in life he would dismiss aerodynamics as a science for people who don't understand engines). But this was also a problematic area in the early years of the "new" Ferrari, for Colombo's V12 required considerable development – and much rancour between the engineers – to deliver respectable horsepower.

Perhaps this accounts for Ferrari's initial reluctance to take on his old firm, Alfa Romeo, head-to-head on the grand prix scene. Ferrari chassis powered by 1.5-litre and 2-litre versions of the Colombo engine, and clad in neatly sculpted bodies

crafted by local coachbuilders, began to pick up victories in the late 1940s.

Most immediately significant was Chinetti's win at the revived Le Mans enduro in 1949, where he drove the majority of the race after his co-driver Lord Selsdon fell ill. And yet, while the Ferrari company of today enjoys flaunting its long association with Formula 1, Ferrari was a notable absentee from the first ever World Championship round, at Silverstone in 1950.

Whether it was the presence of Alfa Romeo – fielding the surviving 158s Ferrari had commissioned Colombo to construct in the late 1930s – or the meagreness of the prize money on offer, Ferrari preferred to concentrate on the Monaco Grand Prix which followed. There the peaky power delivery of the supercharged V12 and dicey handling of the 125 F1 chassis might be less of a disadvantage. Alberto Ascari, whose father had been a racing contemporary of Enzo and had died at the wheel of an Alfa Romeo in 1925, finished second for Ferrari.

BELOW: Monza's newly rebuilt concrete banking formed part of the circuit layout for the 1955 Italian Grand Prix. Ferrari entered six cars (Maurice Trintignant pictured) but were well beaten by Mercedes.

BELOW: Wolfgang von Trips in Ferrari's iconic 156 'Sharknose'.

OPPOSITE: Pole position, fastest lap and race victory in the 1958 French GP earned Ferrari's Mike Hawthorn (4) several bonus cases of champagne from the race promoter.

OVERLEAF: Victory in a Ferrari 250 TR at Le Mans in 1958 set Phil Hill (driving, with Olivier Gendebien) on course for an F1 drive with Ferrari.

Swapping to the Lampredi naturally-aspirated V12 design enabled Ferrari to overturn Alfa Romeo's supremacy and deliver a first World Championship win in 1951, and when the older company hit financial difficulties and withdrew from grand prix racing, Ferrari only had Maserati and, briefly, Lancia as rival national flag bearers. Enzo's sportscars won eight editions of the challenging 1,000-mile Mille Miglia road race and he enjoyed a profitable working relationship with the coachbuilder Pinin Farina in the manufacture of production cars, potential buyers of which were personally vetted by Enzo himself.

14

ABOVE: Phil Hill won the 1961 Italian GP and the world championship, but the race was overshadowed by the death of Hill's team-mate Wolfgang von Trips.

The cars continued to be the stars, while those who designed and raced them were expendable. Perhaps Enzo had developed his armour-plating on the pre-war racing scene as friends and rivals fell. Once engineers had given of their best and began to fail, they fell from favour immediately.

Even Lampredi, whose four-cylinder 2-litre engine enabled Ferrari to dominate the World Championship in 1952–53 – when a shortage of F1 cars led race promoters to court F2 entrants instead – was cast out in 1955, when a larger version failed to cut it as F1 embraced 2.5-litre unblown engines. Enzo had a ready-made replacement in the form of pre-war Alfa Romeo engineer Vittorio Jano, who came part and parcel with the assets of the Lancia D50 project when insolvency forced

Lancia out of racing. Jano contributed a V12 engine which would claim two sportscar world championships and a V6 that would do the same in F1.

Drivers, too, came and went without sentiment, sometimes to their graves. Ascari died testing a Ferrari sportscar at Monza in 1955, bringing Enzo the first of several waves of condemnation from the Vatican and the Italian media. Other deaths, including Alfonso de Portago during the 1957 Mille Miglia and Wolfgang von Trips in the 1961 Italian Grand Prix, brought lengthy legal wrangles as well as further opprobrium

BELOW: The aftermath of the fatal accident on the second lap of the 1961 Italian GP in which Ferrari driver Wolfgang von Trips and 14 spectators died.

OPPOSITE: A tyre blow-out at high speed in the 1957 Mille Miglia had fatal consequences for Alfonso de Portago, co-driver Edmund Nelson, and nine spectators.

from the Pontiff. Trips was Phil Hill's team-mate and rival for that year's Championship and his recollection was that the cars "were never fragile".

"There was, though, something about the ambience at Ferrari that did, indeed, seem to spur drivers to their deaths," recalled Hill. "Perhaps it was the intense sibling-rivalry atmosphere Ferrari fostered, his failure to rank the drivers and his fickleness with the favourites. Luigi Musso died at Rheims, while striving to protect his fair-haired boy status against the encroaching popularity of the Englishmen – Peter Collins and Mike Hawthorn.

"And Peter Collins, a firm favourite… began to get a Ferrari cold shoulder when he married Louise King and went to live aboard a boat in Monte Carlo. Peter was dead within a year."

It's Collins who contributed what is perhaps the most telling piece of eyewitness testimony to Enzo Ferrari's lack of sentimentality towards the people who carried his standard into battle. Collins was in Ferrari's office in March 1957 when the phone rang to inform "The Old Man" that Eugenio Castellotti had died testing a Ferrari F1 car at Modena. Enzo himself had summoned Castellotti from holiday to re-establish a lap record recently broken by Jean Behra in a Maserati.

Enzo – according to Collins – went pale and expressed shock at the news. There then followed a slight pause before he enquired after the health of the car: "*E la macchina?*"

SALE OF THE CENTURY

17
16
DUNLOP

THE ROAD TO SUCCESS

Racing consumed Enzo Ferrari but it had to be paid for, whether through the arcane and unreliable system of negotiating "starting money" (essentially an appearance fee) with promoters, prize money, selling race cars to private entrants... or by selling road cars based on racing underpinnings. In 1948 Ferrari took a stand at the Turin Motor Show and demonstrated two models which electrified both the industry and the public at large.

Collaborating with the Milanese coachbuilder Carrozzeria Touring to append super-light bodywork and luxurious trim to a tube-frame race chassis, Ferrari offered two variations on the 166, a model taking its name from the swept volume in cubic centimetres of a single cylinder in its two-litre Gioachino Colombo-designed V12 engine.

Touring had pioneered and patented the *Superleggera* construction technique of light aluminium panels laid over a web of small-diameter tubing, used to great effect in the Italian aeronautical industry. The open-top 166MM, named after the Mille Miglia road race, connected explicitly with Ferrari's

OPPOSITE: John Surtees (right) frequently complained that sportscar racing diverted resources and focus from Ferrari's Formula 1 programme.

OPPOSITE: To see off the challenge of Ford, Ferrari had 12 cars entered in the 1965 Le Mans 24 Hours. John Surtees (19) co-drove the 330 P2 Spyder with Ludovico Scarfiotti, but gearbox failure ruled the new car out. Masten Gregory and Jochen Rindt won in a Ferrari 250 LM (21) which had qualified 12 seconds off pole position.

BELOW: Surtees won his 1964 world title in a blue and white Ferrari entered by Luigi Chinetti's NART organisation after a dispute between Enzo Ferrari and the Italian sports federation.

successful racing models and its svelte shape compelled the Italian press to describe it as a *barchetta*, meaning "little boat". A year later, Clemente Biondetti drove one to victory at the Mille Miglia, followed by Luigi Chinetti's victory at Le Mans, crystallising the racing connection. Among those rushing to acquire a 166MM was Gianni Agnelli, heir to the Fiat empire among the Agnelli family's other industrial interests.

Alongside the 166MM Ferrari wowed showgoers with another milestone car, the coupé-bodied 166 Inter. Extending the wheelbase enabled the cabin to accommodate a second row of seats for occasional use and it was this, together with the luxuriously appointed interior, which emphasised its intended purpose as a grand tourer rather than a racer. Around 38 were built via Ferrari's customary method, typical of the day, whereby naked chassis were delivered to a coachbuilder and finished in a body of the client's choice.

Enzo, mindful of his enterprise's mystique, vetted each potential buyer personally; such gatekeeping merely encouraged

OIL
FERODO
GIRLING
SHELL SHELL
21
19

ABOVE: The 250 GT Coupé Pinin Farina was the first road-going Ferrari to be built in substantial numbers.

the wealthy, famous and well-heeled to his door. Among the first customers was Prince Igor Troubetzkoy, fourth of Woolworth heiress Barbara Hutton's seven husbands. He co-drove with Biondetti in an Allemano-bodied 166 to win the Targa Florio in May 1948.

Perhaps the most prolific Ferrari purchaser of the 1950s was Porfirio Rubirosa, a polo player and racing driver whom many believe to have been involved in political black-bag operations – including assassinations – on behalf of Dominican dictator Rafael Trujillo. He was also Hutton's fifth husband, albeit for only 53 days, and dated a string of stars including Marilyn Monroe, Rita Hayworth, Eartha Kitt, Joan Crawford, Ava Gardner and Zsa Zsa Gabor (who accompanied him to Le Mans in 1954, only for Rubirosa's team-mate to crash their 375 MM on the fifth lap). Rubirosa met his maker after wrapping his 250 GT around a tree in the Bois de Boulogne, having spent the evening celebrating a polo

BELOW: Though built for the road, the 250 GT Coupé Pinin Farina had enough in common with racing Ferraris to be put through its paces in competition.

victory. Associations with famous rogues did Ferrari's profile no harm at all.

Ferrari's most profitable collaboration with a coachbuilder, before gravitating from the artisan construction model, came with Pinin Farina. Founded in Turin in 1930 by Battista "Pinin" Farina, and renamed with a single-word spelling in 1961 after his sons Sergio and Renzo took over the business, the company established its credentials with a series of smoothly sculpted Alfa Romeo and Lancia-based specials in the pre-war era. Farina-bodied Ferrari road cars powered by the F1-derived long-block Aurelio Lampredi V12 helped launch the marque in America.

LUCAS
SOLEX
POLAROIL
DUNLOP
DUNLOP
POLAROIL
EYQUEM
34
34
GB 3000 RW
35
35
GB 3001 RW

From the early 1950s through to the 1960s, a succession of models featuring a three-litre version of the Colombo V12 and bearing the 250 designation (each cylinder being 250cc) seamlessly blended hand-crafted elegance with race-bred technology. Racers including the 250 TR won the Le Mans 24 Hours four times and clocked up three victories in the 12 Hours of Sebring. On the road, the likes of the 250 GT California gained traction with movie stars, while the 250 GT Coupé was the first Ferrari to be built in any great number – more than 350 left the factory.

But the sudden ramping up of production offered a clue to the turbulence behind the scenes if one cared to look deeper. By the early 1960s, the company was being pulled in many different directions. Enzo's policy of ruling his empire from the centre, relying on trusted lieutenants to feed him information, left him open to manipulation and meant he lost touch with what was really happening at the cutting edge. In Formula 1, rival British teams Enzo dismissed as "mere garagistes" profited by relocating the engine to the rear of the chassis for better balance, and following more modern aerospace construction practice to save weight.

Thanks to the power of the "Dino" V6 engine (named after Enzo's deceased son, who is said to have proposed it), Ferrari's Mike Hawthorn narrowly won the F1 drivers' championship in 1958. Ferrari won both drivers' and constructors' titles in 1961 – but only because a smaller version of the Dino engine was ready when racing's governing body slashed the maximum displacement to 1.5 litres.

LEFT: The Le Mans 24 Hours, one of the most arduous and prestigious races in the world, offered a great sales platform for Ferrari sportscars.

LEFT: Through the 1960s Ferrari offered a range of mid-engined cars powered by modest V6 engines, badged as "Dino" after his dead son. The Dino 246 GT was a very capable rival for Porsche's 911.

None of the British teams had an answer until later, whereupon they left Ferrari standing. Innovative low-weight, high-strength chassis design and low-profile aerodynamics would define the competitive order in this era and Ferrari's "Sharknose" 156, while pretty, had little going for it apart from its looks and its engine. The 1961 Monaco Grand Prix, where Stirling Moss danced clear in an obsolete Lotus from the pursuing 156s of Phil Hill and Richie Ginther, should have been taken as an augury.

At the end of 1961, a group of senior staff, including engineer Carlo Chiti and team manager Romolo Tavoni, walked out en masse. Since Dino's death in 1956, Enzo's wife Laura had taken to attending the factory more regularly and staging interventions in matters of policy. Her forthright manner put noses out of joint; Enzo, Chiti would recall, "allowed her to get away with a great deal – possibly too much – because she was the mother of his son". Other behind-the-scenes issues contributed to a souring of the atmosphere, and the death of Wolfgang von Trips in a Ferrari at the Italian Grand Prix led to the inevitable thunder of disapproval from the Vatican.

Widespread industrial unrest in Italy meant supply shortages, and this held back Ferrari from increasing production at a time when the company's finances were under pressure. Laura's presence in the factory jeopardised the careful separation Enzo had established between his different lives, including supporting his mistress and their son. Little wonder that, having passed his 60th birthday, he took refuge in entertaining the desires of his famous customers while considering a partial sale of his company to an outsider.

This was the scene which greeted John Surtees when Enzo recruited him in 1963. Already a champion on two wheels and possessing a willpower as steely as his knuckle-crushing

OPPOSITE: As he entered his 60s, Enzo Ferrari began to consider selling the company that bore his name.

20

handshake, "*Il Grande John*" spoke Italian and was well-versed in the political nature of the country's industry having ridden for MV Agusta. Nevertheless he immediately cultivated a dislike for Tavoni's replacement, Eugenio Dragoni, while forming a good working relationship with new chief engineer Mauro Forghieri.

Dragoni was already wealthy from other business interests and the chief item on his manifesto was to provide Ferrari – and the country – with an Italian-born world champion. 27-year-old Forghieri's internship at the company had been facilitated by his father, Reclus, a longtime Ferrari employee who had installed the first foundry at Maranello. Now Forghieri junior was persuaded to set aside his hopes of working for Lockheed in the US, and focus on chassis as well as engine development at Ferrari.

Forghieri's youthful energy proved vital in this febrile period while resources were stretched. He led the design on the spaceframe-chassis P-series sports prototypes which finished 1–2–3 at Le Mans in 1964, laid out a new 1.5-litre flat-12 F1 engine, and overhauled the troubled 156. While the latter had mixed results, Forghieri's "Aero" chassis concept aped certain elements of the British cars, such as placing the driver in a more reclined position and using areas of bodywork as load-bearing parts of the structure.

Surtees claimed the F1 world title – just – at the final round of 1964 in Forghieri's new 158, but bugbears continued to abound. The Englishman felt that no meaningful work on the F1 cars was done until after Le Mans, and that Dragoni was forcing him to use new and unproven developments, while the Italian drivers got the best machinery available. The simmering rancour came to a head at Le Mans in 1966 against a broader canvas of Ferrari facing off against Ford.

OPPOSITE: When Formula 1 adopted three-litre engines in 1966, Ferrari lacked resources to build a bespoke engine and had to use a sportscar-derived V12 which was heavy and lacked power.

RIGHT: Ford finally toppled Ferrari at Le Mans in 1966. The highest-placed Ferrari, in eighth, was a privately entered 275 GTB driven by Piers Courage and Roy Pike (29).

During 1963, the US giant had come within a few key contractual paragraphs of acquiring a major stake in Ferrari. Unfortunately, the offending sentences concerned who would have control over the racing budget. Enzo was prepared to abdicate control over his road cars, but not his beloved racing division and walked out on the Ford delegation, prompting Henry Ford II to declare war. Le Mans was the chosen battleground.

Come 1966, Surtees was fuming that his new F1 car wasn't up to scratch; the formula had changed again, to three-litre engines, but there was no budget to develop a new one, so the F1 project had to make do with a sleeved-down version of the sportscar engine. It was too heavy and not powerful enough. Then, at Le Mans, Dragoni partnered Surtees with Ludovico Scarfiotti – Gianni Agnelli's nephew – and directed that Scarfiotti take the first stint behind the wheel. It was a clear

BELOW: Lorenzo Bandini's fatal accident at Monaco in 1967 put an end to the practice of using straw bales as trackside impact protection.

OPPOSITE: Powered by a new flat-12 engine, the 312B briefly revived Ferrari's F1 fortunes in 1970.

political play, since Agnelli was in attendance and Fiat was now the leading candidate to buy Ferrari.

"Do you want to win this race or not?" thundered Surtees, who stormed out, never to race a Ferrari again. Scarfiotti crashed out during the night and Ford cantered to a 1–2–3 finish.

This was a troubling period indeed for Ferrari as Ford's success in sportscar racing jeopardised one of the company's most lucrative profit centres, and the F1 project continued to disappoint. Lorenzo Bandini's death at Monaco in 1967 cast a further pall over Ferrari's fortunes. In June 1969 Enzo agreed to sell 40 per cent of the business to Fiat, which granted his wish of retaining control over all racing activities.

The following years would bring many challenges, but now keeping the company alive would not be among them.

GLORY AND POWER

GOODYEAR
Marlboro
GOODYEAR
Agip
HEUER
12
GOODYEAR

REBUILDING THE LEGEND

Fiat's investment in 1969 stabilised Ferrari's finances and provided large-scale manufacturer expertise which would prove vital to the company's growth in the road car market. It also enabled Enzo Ferrari to provide for his illegitimate son, Piero, who was given a 10 per cent shareholding; Enzo retained control over sporting matters as well as a 50 per cent holding which would revert to Fiat upon his death. But difficult decisions lay ahead on track, where the Ferrari legend was born, nurtured and sustained.

These decisions would involve confronting an uncomfortable truth John Surtees had voiced years earlier: that Ferrari were trying to compete on too many fronts and lacked the resources to do so, especially when building engines as well as cars.

Changes on the sportscar racing scene were beginning to starve Ferrari's table of its bread and butter. During the 1960s iconic cars such as the 250 GTO proved marvellously lucrative, winning in the hands of Ferrari's own works team and selling to wealthy private entrants. But race promoters increasingly wanted more spectacle and star quality, demanding more

OPPOSITE: Niki Lauda brought technical savvy and a no-nonsense attitude to the F1 team – and claimed two world championships.

ABOVE: Ferrari fitted a long tail section to the 512 S at Le Mans in 1970 to reduce drag. Ronnie Bucknum and Sam Posey finished fourth, behind three Porsches.

of the high-powered sports-prototypes whose cost and performance were too much for most gentlemen racers. GT cars were declared ineligible for the world championship. The sports-prototype scene became a battle of manufacturers, one in which Ferrari was regularly bested by Ford and Porsche, despite the governing body's attempts to cap performance by insisting each car maker had to build a set minimum number of examples for sale.

Before yielding to the inevitable and quitting sportscars in 1973, Ferrari took the battle to Porsche and its mighty – if hairy – 917. Among the first beneficiaries of the Fiat deal was the 512 S, developed by Mauro Forghieri's engineering team in just a handful of months with the aim of beating the 917s at Le Mans in June 1970.

That January, Ferrari presented the necessary 25 finished cars to FIA officials at Maranello: powered by a five-litre V12

BELOW: A transversely mounted gearbox which improved weight distribution helped make the 312T a winner in Formula 1.

cradled in a semi-monocoque steel-and-aluminium chassis, it was a slightly heavier proposition than the 917 with its air-cooled flat-12 and spindly spaceframe. The balance of power remained with Porsche, although Mario Andretti scored a memorable victory in the Sebring 12 Hours, reeling in and passing an older Porsche 908 driven by Peter Revson and movie star Steve McQueen after the 917s failed. McQueen then acquired one of the modified "M" models of the 512 for his film *Le Mans*.

Fiat's money also lubricated final development on Forghieri's new three-litre flat-12 engine, enabling it to progress from promising failure into a unit which would carry the Maranello torch at the top level of motorsport for a full decade. It would be a faltering path back to greatness, though. Armed with the new flat-12-powered 312B, Jacky Ickx won three grands prix in 1970 and finished second in the World Championship despite retiring from six rounds. Team-mate Clay Regazzoni also delighted the home fans with victory at Monza but, thereafter, Ferrari began to slip back into a trough.

Why was this? As well as the division of resources to sportscar racing, there was the reporting structure which enabled Enzo to enjoy his philosophy of being "an agitator of men", fostering creative tension, but which also kept him remote from reality.

British teams had long since embraced full monocoque construction in which the car's bodywork is integral to the structure rather than a cosmetic addition and Ford's DFV V8 made it possible for the engine to be bolted directly to the chassis and form part of the structure after 1967. Ferrari, however, persisted with a semi-monocoque chassis in which the engine, gearbox and rear suspension were supported by subframes, a

heavier and less efficient configuration.

The DFV's affordability made it almost ubiquitous in Formula 1 in the 1970s, forcing teams to innovate in aerodynamics and chassis technology to find an edge. Tyre manufacturers got in on the act; Ferrari were the first F1 team to use treadless "slick" rubber, in 1971. After going up a number of blind alleys, Forghieri was briefly banished to "special projects" as Enzo lost faith in him, the tipping point coming when Ickx turned his nose up at the unusual-looking 312B3 in testing and the Italian press hooted with derision at the *spazzaneve* – literally "snowplough".

BELOW: Designer Mauro Forghieri tried a short wheelbase and side-mounted radiators in the 1973 312B3, but the car – likened to a snowplough by the press – went unraced.

ABOVE: Ferrari's new sporting director, the urbane, educated, ambitious Luca di Montezemolo (left) formed a strong working partnership with Niki Lauda (right).

As a measure of the desperation involved, Forghieri's replacement Sandro Colombo began a new 312B3 from a clean sheet, approaching the specialist British metalworking company TC Prototypes to construct a monocoque because the expertise to do this did not exist at Maranello. It was a brave move, but the car failed to deliver results. The crunch came at the 1973 British Grand Prix where Ickx qualified 19th, more than two seconds off the pole position time, and finished only eighth even though nine other cars were eliminated in a crash on the opening lap.

The farce prompted rapid changes. Enzo withdrew his cars from the following rounds, recalled Forghieri, and charged new sporting director Luca di Montezemolo with the task of finding a new star driver to replace Ickx, who had indicated he no longer wished to race a Ferrari again. Niki Lauda emerged as the prime candidate although, upon sampling the B3 for the first time, the straight-talking young Austrian had to be coached by Piero not to tell Enzo that his car was a basket case.

Like Surtees before him, Lauda gelled with Forghieri and had a gift for car development. Together they chiselled away at the B3 and Forghieri totally remodelled the cooling system along the lines of the recent championship-winning Lotus and Tyrrell cars, putting the radiators ahead of the rear wheels to concentrate weight in the middle of the car. In 1974 it was a

LEFT: Enzo Ferrari (left) delighted in the turnaround in form on track after recruiting Lauda (centre) and Clay Regazzoni (right).

BELOW: Weeks after suffering severe burns at the Nürburgring, Niki Lauda (right) declared himself fit to race again at Monza... but found Ferrari had hired Carlos Reutemann (left) to replace him, requiring the team to enter a third car.

race-winner again and only a series of retirements eliminated Lauda from the title chase. Team-mate Clay Regazzoni finished a narrow second to McLaren's Emerson Fittipaldi.

For 1975 Forghieri designed an all-new chassis, the 312T, with a transverse gearbox to yield even better weight distribution. After initial reservations – why change when the old car was competitive enough? – Lauda won five races and the world title.

He might have won again in 1976 but for a fiery accident at the Nürburgring in which he nearly died. Six weeks after receiving the last rites, Lauda was back in the cockpit at the Italian Grand Prix to the surprise of everybody, not least Carlos Reutemann, who had been hired to replace him. Lauda was still in contention for the title when he withdrew from the final

ABOVE: The 126C2 was Ferrari's first monocoque car to be built in-house. At Long Beach in 1982 it featured this unusual double rear wing – Ferrari's means of protesting at British teams getting away with what they saw as cheating.

round in Japan, deeming the wet conditions suicidally unsafe. He was castigated as a coward by the Italian press but not by Enzo, who remembered his own crisis of confidence at the wheel more than 60 years earlier.

The 1976 F1 season was the first to be widely televised and the dramatic title battle between Lauda and James Hunt seized the imagination of the global public. Forghieri's 312T series delivered two more world championships, one for Lauda and one for Jody Scheckter, although aerodynamic innovations enabled the British teams to take the initiative once again in a way Ferrari were unable to follow.

To cope with the changing times Ferrari would have to embrace turbocharging, monocoque construction and carbonfibre – seismic changes for a company whose ethos sprang from artisan metalwork. The company's first in-house monocoque, the 126C2, earned Ferrari the constructors' title in 1982, a season marred by off-track politics and on-track tragedy. Enzo delighted in the former, cementing himself in a

Agip
Marlboro
WORLD CHAMPIONSHIP TEAM
CHAMPION
SMEG

position of influence as the British teams formed a negotiating bloc against the governing body; but he was grievously wounded by the latter.

The incandescent driving talent of Gilles Villeneuve made him a fan favourite and Enzo's darling. The Old Man had long since developed an armour plating where driver injury and death was concerned, and yet he was hit hard by Villeneuve's death in an accident during qualifying for the Belgian GP. "He made Ferrari a household name and I was very fond of him," he said. One round earlier, Villeneuve and team-mate Didier Pironi had clashed over team orders at San Marino, where Pironi passed Villeneuve late on to win. They were still not speaking when Gilles met his end. Later in the season Pironi broke both legs in a crash in Germany and never drove an F1 car again.

OPPOSITE: French-Canadian ace Gilles Villeneuve delighted Enzo Ferrari and the team's fans with his bravura approach to racing.

BELOW: Ferrari's first turbo car, the 126CK, was slow and handled badly, but Villeneuve scored a memorable victory in it at Monaco in 1981.

ABOVE: Built to celebrate Ferrari's 40th anniversary, the F40 brought F1 technology to the road and remains one of the company's most desirable and iconic cars.

In 1983 Ferrari again won the constructors' championship but not the drivers' crown. As McLaren rose to prominence with a series of highly advanced and fuel-efficient cars, Enzo decided to make their designer, John Barnard, an offer he couldn't refuse. And yet refuse Barnard did, until granted a remarkable concession: that he could set up a new design and construction facility in England.

Ferrari celebrated 40 years in business in 1987 with the

remarkable limited edition F40 supercar – designed at the behest of Enzo, who felt the company's road car range was growing stale and pedestrian. The F40 was a four-wheeled response to Porsche's 959, a brutally minimalist race car for the road. It was also the last Ferrari to be signed off for production by Enzo before his death in August 1988.

Enzo's final months were turbulent. It's said that what he most feared as his health declined was losing his memory.

OVERLEAF: McLaren dominated the 1988 season, but Ferrari's Gerhard Berger and Michele Alboreto finished 1-2 at the Italian Grand Prix three weeks after Enzo Ferrari's death.

Bevete
Coca-Cola
Coke
Agip
2
1

Bevete
Coca-Cola
Coke
LANCIA
PRISMA
LANCIA
Agip

And yet he was trenchant to the last. When it was discovered that Barnard's new F1 car, aimed to be a technological tour de force, had been put behind schedule because a rival faction, led by Piero, had been using Maranello's windtunnel resources to design a car of their own, Enzo came down on the side of his superstar engineer and banished Piero to the road car division.

McLaren won every grand prix in 1988 except one. Three weeks after Enzo's death, Gerhard Berger and Michele Alboreto finished 1–2 for Ferrari – at Monza, of all places, amidst the whispering trees of the royal park where it's said the spirits of departed Italian racing greats walk. Nuvolari, Ascari, and now Enzo Ferrari.

OPPOSITE: Enzo Ferrari suffered from diabetes in later life and died at the age of 90.

BELOW: Monza was the scene of a remarkable win for the Scuderia after Ferrari's death in August 1988.

THE PRICE OF PROGRESS

GOODYEAR
Agip
1
GOODYEAR
GOODYEAR

FORWARDS, NOT BACK

"*Non mi piacciono i monumenti*", Enzo Ferrari once said. "I don't like monuments." And yet the marque which continues to bear his name is precisely that, a moving symphony in *Rosso Corsa*, for all that it tries to look forwards, not back.

That was always the Ferrari way. Very few of the racing cars from the 1950s and 1960s survive, except those which made their way into private hands. Works cars, even the magical, championship-winning ones – the ex-Lancia D50s, the Dino 246s, the "Sharknose" 156s – were unsentimentally cannibalised, modified and/or recycled. Always the focus was on the next race. While there are those who say that in his waning years Enzo took less interest in the business – and perhaps on the road car side, Fiat's bailiwick, that was so – he continued to attend his office in the centre of the Fiorano test track until he was no longer strong enough to stand.

It's this passion which has made Ferrari virtually a second religion in Italy, and enabled the company to survive while

OPPOSITE: The 641 was beautiful as well as ground-breaking – one is on display at New York's Museum of Modern Art.

OPPOSITE: Poached from McLaren and given a free hand, John Barnard brought an uncompromising technical vision to Ferrari.

similar enterprises have failed. Enzo's death was a pivotal moment in Ferrari's history, a moment of existential crisis – but, amid the chaos of the aftermath of his passing, skilled and strong-willed characters emerged to preserve the magic while looking to the future.

What Ferrari needed was success on the track and more volume in road car sales. In Formula 1, Enzo had hired the most gifted and visionary engineer of his generation: John Barnard, "*Il Mago*" (the magician) to the Italian press, "prince of darkness" to those who tested his patience. The working arrangements – Barnard's team designing and prototyping from an office near Godalming and faxing schematics to Maranello for manufacture – were imperfect. Michele Alboreto likened it to performing brain surgery down the telephone.

For all the politics and Maranello sabotage, though – largely quashed after Enzo purged the dissidents, including his own son – Barnard's new Ferrari would turn out to be a work of art. While the engine department disliked being dictated to by an outsider, especially a perfectionist one with a short fuse, the idea of going back to a naturally aspirated V12 wasn't unwelcome.

Motor racing's governing body, the FIA, sealed the deal by outlawing turbocharged engines ahead of the 1989 season. Barnard's key innovation, one present in the majority of Ferraris today as well as countless other cars, was born of imagining how to eliminate one of a race car designer's principal bugbears: how to package the gearshift mechanism.

In 1964, John Surtees cured the problem of his hand being too big to slip between the gear lever and the chassis by whacking the bulkhead out with a lump hammer. In the late 1980s, the problem facing Barnard was that aerodynamic priorities called for a narrow cockpit, and there was very little space to accommodate the gearshift comfortably alongside the

BELOW: Gerhard Berger was a race winner, and a fan favourite, during two stints with Ferrari in the 1980s and 1990s.

driver. Creating a "blister" to leave room for the gear lever to move – essentially doing via a moulding what Surtees did with a hammer – was considered inefficient and inelegant. There was also the perennial problem of routing the shifting mechanism out through the back of a load-bearing structure, past the engine, to the gearbox. Changing gears electro-pneumatically, via levers mounted behind the steering wheel, did away with all that and enabled the driver to change gear without taking their hand off the wheel.

Unfortunately, the semi-automatic system was bedevilled by reliability glitches which proved hard to pin down. Barnard's gorgeously sculpted 640 car would run competitively quickly for a handful of laps before halting. At the first grand prix of the 1989 season, in Rio, team manager Cesare Fiorio wanted drivers Gerhard Berger and Nigel Mansell to start with barely any fuel on board so they could at least lead the race before

they inevitably stopped. Seemingly against the odds Mansell won, even though the bolts holding his steering wheel in place worked loose.

It would be another three months and six grands prix before either Ferrari finished a race again, during which time the theory that the gearbox was the source of the problems became inked into the public consciousness. In fact, vibrations through the engine's crankshaft threw off the alternator belt and killed the electrics.

In 1990 Alain Prost joined Ferrari from McLaren and pushed his old nemesis Ayrton Senna closely for the championship, until Senna had a moment of madness in Japan and drove Prost (and himself) off the road at 180 mph. After Barnard had left for another team, his successors struggled to develop the concept, so 1991 was a disappointing season, and

ABOVE: Alain Prost brought the number one to Ferrari in 1990 but fell just short of the drivers' title.

Prost was fired before the end of it for making critical remarks about the car. Some aspects of life at Ferrari never change…

For all Ferrari's yo-yo performances on track, mystique continued to inhabit its road cars even though some models – the front-engined V12 grand tourers in particular – lacked appeal to the younger demographic. Others, while iconic, were unattainable and already long in the tooth as the 1980s drew to a close.

The mid-engined flat-12 Testarossa, for instance, was essentially a rebodied and re-engineered version of the 512 BB, which had first seen the light of day in 1973. Customers hadn't liked the way the ducting for the front-mounted radiators made the cockpit hot; in relocating the radiators to the flanks and

feeding them with dramatic-looking side streaks, the engineers and stylists perfectly captured the emergent "look-at-me vibe" of the 1980s. While the Testarossa was too wide, and its handling at the limit too unruly, to be considered a proper performance car by purists, sheer desirability ensured demand outstripped Ferrari's production capacity.

Similarly the pretty, Pininfarina-styled and V8-powered 328, though a big seller, was an evolution of the 308 first introduced in 1975, and the influential motoring press was beginning to point out that rival manufacturers' cars were better. The 348, launched in 1989, offered little that was new, except Testarossa styling cues.

Global economic recession, rising oil prices and changing

BELOW: While many of the 348 Spider's underpinnings dated from the 1970s, its streaked sides perfectly caught the ostentatious vibe of the 1980s.

ABOVE: A world champion with the Scuderia in 1975 and 1977, Niki Lauda returned as a consultant in the 1990s.

social attitudes had an ossifying effect on performance car sales. Conspicuous consumption briefly ceased to be fashionable. The waiting list for the Testarossa – one which speculators were willing to pay up to double the asking price in order to jump – melted away like April snow. Debts began to accumulate as the F1 team's wobbly performances impacted the balance sheet.

Enzo's death had left a power vacuum, with all the petty manoeuvrings that entailed. Another strong leader was required and, to that end, Fiat magnate Gianni Agnelli installed former sporting director Luca di Montezemolo as president, with the twin aims of restoring sales and rebooting the flagship F1 racing programme.

When the suave, urbane Montezemolo first arrived at Maranello in 1973, fresh out of university, there were those who wondered what family connections he enjoyed to have been elevated so quickly to a position of such responsibility. Now, after a successful career in Italian industry and sport – including a role in the Italia '90 football World Cup – there was no doubting his credentials.

Montezemolo rehired Niki Lauda, twice a world champion with Ferrari, as a consultant, and they quickly realised change was needed in the F1 project. The radical but flawed F92A car was evidence of a chaotic design programme: the aerodynamic benefits of its twin-floor design were highly theoretical and untested in the field. Sure enough, the aero loads were super-sensitive to changes in pitch under acceleration and braking.

BELOW: The F92A looked fantastic, but its daring twin-floor aerodynamic concept didn't work in practice

With an active suspension system like the one on the rival Williams car, it might have worked, but Ferrari's equivalent was late and unreliable, and added weight to the car. The new V12 engine lacked power and was prone to oil starvation in corners, something new recruit Ivan Capelli pointed out, only to be directed to shut up – because team-mate Jean Alesi was raving about how great the engine was.

The enormity of the task ahead was brought home in 1992. Realising the jobs of revitalising the racing and road car division was too much for one person, Montezemolo hired

former rally co-driver Jean Todt from Peugeot's sportscar programme to head up Ferrari's *Gestione Sportiva*. Lauda, who won his last world title at the wheel of a Barnard-designed car, set to work luring the legendary engineer back into the fold.

Barnard's svelte 412T1 car wowed the excitable Italian media, which likened it to "a pebble washed by the sea". Its innovative cooling system proved troublesome, though, since – according to Barnard – the engine department had got its calculations wrong. Several months were lost to mutual recriminations but, after several revisions, the car returned

ABOVE: John Barnard's 412T1 made Ferrari winners again but its cooling architecture required a lot of debugging first.

BELOW: Though its looks harked back to previous mid-engined V8 Ferraris, the F355 was a huge improvement on its predecessors in terms of quality and everyday driveability.

Ferrari to the winners' circle at the German Grand Prix in 1994.

That year was also significant on the road for Ferrari, as the F355 replaced the moribund 348. Styled again by Pininfarina, its shape and detailing evoked the classic 288GTO and 308GTB without lapsing into pastiche. Multi-valve heads and advanced materials enabled the high-revving 3.5-litre V8 to produce more power per litre than any of its rivals and yet the car had impeccable manners on the road. It was the most civilised Ferrari yet, despite its incredible performance potential. More than 11,000 units had hit the road by the time it was superseded five years later.

Ferrari also established a profitable sideline in US sportscar racing as it designed and built – with the aid of subcontractors – the 333SP sports prototype. Proposed by Gianpiero Moretti, founder of the MOMO aftermarket components company, championed by Enzo's son Piero, and part-realised by former Ferrari engineer Gian Paolo Dallara's company, the 333SP won 12 significant sportscar championships in its lifetime.

And yet consistent success in Formula 1 continued to prove elusive, prompting Jean Todt to begin sweeping changes – both in the cockpit and in the design office.

RIGHT: Ferrari's first sports-prototype in over 20 years, the 333SP, was a great success in US sportscar racing.

88
GRAND-AM
GOODYEAR
SYMBOLIC
333sp
.com
ROLEX

THE SCHUMACHER YEARS

THE MASTER ARRIVES

From the mid-1990s onwards, the elements which would bring about a renaissance in Ferrari's fortunes on road and track began to slot into place. On the second Sunday of June 1995, plucky Jean Alesi – a favourite of the Ferrari *tifosi*, and seen very much as the heir to Gilles Villeneuve – won the Canadian Grand Prix in John Barnard's handsome 412T2 F1.

Superstitiously inclined fans saw it as an augury: Alesi was celebrating his birthday and carrying the number 27, Villeneuve's race number, on his car – at a circuit named in honour of Villeneuve. Sadly, it would be Alesi's only F1 victory.

Less sentimental, more pragmatic business was brewing behind the scenes. Newly hired engine chief Paolo Martinelli was thinking the unthinkable, plotting the end of the V12 engine synonymous with Ferrari's brand. Amid a host of changes introduced to cut car performance in the wake of Ayrton Senna's tragic death at Imola in 1994, the FIA had reduced the maximum engine displacement from 3.5 litres to three. Exotic materials, more advanced lubricants and high-

OPPOSITE: Michael Schumacher's ability and work ethic proved transformative when he arrived at Maranello.

BELOW: Jean Todt had been a rally co-driver and his early years with Ferrari were just as much of a white-knuckle ride

tech design resources now enabled V10 engines to rev as highly as V12s and match them for power, while weighing less and having fewer moving parts to fail or suffer frictional losses.

And on the very weekend of Alesi's triumph, rumours began to circulate that reigning world champion Michael Schumacher was on his way to Maranello. The rumours were somewhat premature, but turned out to be correct. Team principal Jean Todt, along with Schumacher and his manager and Ferrari's lawyer, met in a Monte Carlo hotel a month later. Fearful of being observed, they furtively relocated to Schumacher's apartment and it was there, hidden away from prying eyes, they put pen to contractual paper for the 1996 season.

Being a Ferrari driver exerts a special pull. For Schumacher this was both a new challenge and an opportunity to put space between himself and his soon-to-be-former team, Benetton, who were widely believed to have cheated during 1994, his first championship year. FIA investigations had discovered illegal traction control functions hidden in Benetton's software, but the governing body hadn't been able to establish beyond doubt that they had actually been used.

Reliability continued to be a disappointment and Alesi's victory plus a handful of other podium finishes were all Ferrari could take from the season. Schumacher was coming on the promise that change was around the corner but, when the first batch of V10 engines proved fragile, as an insurance policy a V12-engined 412T2 was packed into the truck for a post-season test at Portugal's Estoril circuit. In it, the newly crowned

ABOVE: Schumacher was remarkable in the 1996 Spanish Grand Prix, circulating three seconds a lap faster than his nearest rivals in the wet.

double world champion lapped a second quicker than either Alesi or Gerhard Berger had managed in the Portuguese Grand Prix at the same venue during the summer. In public he merely acknowledged the car was "very, very good", but in private – according to Barnard – he said, "I could have won the world championship much more easily with this car..."

The first car designed to accommodate a V10, the F310, proved to be something of a misstep as Barnard's design team overlooked a number of obvious regulatory loopholes in their

LEFT: Teething troubles with Ferrari's first V10-powered F1 car, the F310, prompted a significant change in the team's technical philosophy.

search for unusual and radical solutions. New regulations dictated higher cockpit padding to improve driver safety, and the F310's cockpit padding was faithful to the spirit of the rules, while rival designers exploited the wording to minimise potential aerodynamic blockages in this area.

Vibrations from the new engine cracked the gearbox casing, forcing Ferrari to revert to a previous design which had different pick-up points for the suspension wishbones, forcing another compromise. Poor form and reliability

BELOW: Schumacher was stripped of his championship points after hitting title rival Jacques Villeneuve in the 1997 European Grand Prix.

OPPOSITE: Ferrari poached technical director Ross Brawn from Benetton with a mandate to transform operations at Maranello.

early in the season led to calls in the Italian media for Todt to be sacked, and the shrieking abated only briefly when Schumacher claimed a sensational wet-weather victory in the Spanish Grand Prix at the Circuit de Catalunya.

Schumacher made it known that if Todt was forced out, he would follow, but this high-profile backing would only buy a little time. It was time to put an end to the peculiar arrangement in which the car designs were faxed from the UK to Italy one page at a time. Barnard declined to move to Italy, so Todt needed to install a whole new design facility, which he achieved by poaching technical director Ross Brawn and chief designer Rory Byrne from Benetton, courtesy of an introduction furnished by Schumacher.

Lacking substantial resources to begin with, and not just in terms of staff – Ferrari's wind tunnel was well out of date – they developed the F310 into a B-spec for 1997. Schumacher won five grands prix in it and put himself in contention for the title, but was stripped of his points for trying to ram his championship rival, Jacques Villeneuve, off the track in the final round.

vodafone

Marlboro
Marlboro
GRAN PREM
ARLBORO
ARGENTINA
S AIRES 1998
Shell
GOODYEAR
Marlboro
OMP
Marlboro

The upward trajectory continued as Todt's appointees formed an increasingly powerful fighting unit, with Todt in effect acting as a firewall to shield them from internal politics and the rabid Italian media. One of Brawn's first acts was to ban newspapers from the technical office as he felt too much time and energy was being wasted reading and worrying about what outsiders thought of the job they were doing.

Brawn also acted to remove the parochial thinking and petty inter-departmental rivalries, encouraging round-table discussions in which all attendees were invited to conjure ideas which might provide fractional gains. Taken together, Brawn assured them, these tiny gains would accumulate into big ones.

Throughout 1998 and '99 the revitalised team firmly established their status as F1's second force behind McLaren, who had the fastest car but not always the most reliable one. Schumacher was second to McLaren's Mika Häkkinen in 1998, but missed almost half of the 1999 season after breaking his leg at the British Grand Prix.

Team-mate Eddie Irvine pushed Häkkinen close, and helped Ferrari to win the constructors' title. The key difference between the teams was that McLaren had a competitive car straight out of the box, even if it occasionally broke, whereas Ferrari had discovered durability but required lots of in-season development to match their rivals' speed.

The year of the big push was 2000, aided by the newly built wind tunnel which was installed, in a huge statement of intent, at the eastern gate of the Maranello campus in a grandiose building designed by the celebrated architect Renzo Piano.

Todt was insistent that his team had to redouble their efforts and start strong. After an epic season-long duel with Häkkinen, the balance shifting almost from race to race, Schumacher sealed the title with one round to go in Japan. It was Ferrari's first drivers' championship in 21 years, and Schumacher

OPPOSITE: Schumacher's 'victory leap' on the podium became a common sight in the early 2000s.

ABOVE: The F2002 enabled Schumacher to secure his third consecutive drivers' title with six rounds of the 2002 season remaining.

emphasised that this was no transient fluke by winning the last four rounds from pole position.

Over the next four seasons Schumacher brought his total of championships to a record-breaking seven and Ferrari established an unparalleled and virtually unchallenged position of technical dominance. The F2002 and F2004 rank among the most successful grand prix cars of all time (indeed, more than 15 years later, the F2004 still holds race lap records at Albert Park, Shanghai International Circuit and Monza). Of the 85 grands prix contested between 2000 and 2004, Ferrari won 57 and appeared on the podium of 23 others, as well as claiming 51 pole positions and recording 42 fastest laps.

This relentless success was founded upon an absence of complacency. Even after a resounding victory, Todt and Brawn habitually gathered senior staff to forensically analyse the race and identify possible improvements. They never took anything for granted, as evidenced by the 2002 Austrian Grand Prix, round six of 17, where Schumacher's team-mate Rubens Barrichello was ordered to move over and hand victory to Michael. Every point counted.

Inevitably, this run of success prompted mutterings of disquiet in the corridors of power. Rival teams tried to copy Ferrari's designs but failed to come close, so they lobbied for change, as did the commercial rights holder, who fretted that global TV audiences were becoming fatigued by repetition. Rule changes were introduced to peg Ferrari back.

This period of dominance also sprinkled stardust on the balance sheet as the F1 team became a net contributor to Ferrari's profits rather than a drain on them – and not a moment too soon, since parent company Fiat had hit financial turbulence. The halo effect of burgeoning excellence on track, allied to Schumacher's star power, fed a golden period of

BELOW: Fans booed during the podium ceremony of the 2002 Austrian GP after Rubens Barrichello (centre) was ordered to hand over the lead to Schumacher.

OVERLEAF: The F430 brought a fresh look to Ferrari's model range as well as a lightweight aluminium construction.

ABOVE: Returning to the front-mounted V12 template for its grand tourers with the 550 Maranello, Ferrari created a better-handling car than the mid-engined models it replaced.

road car sales as new models decisively blew away some of the lingering weaknesses of old.

The F50, built to celebrate the company's 50th anniversary, was the first road-going Ferrari not to employ the traditional fundamentals of a tube-frame chassis. Based on a carbon fibre monocoque and powered by a 4.7-litre V12 engine derived from the one used in the 640 F1 car, it genuinely brought Formula 1 technology to the road. Ferrari's volume models were also transformed: the 360 Modena, which replaced the F355 in 1999, featured a larger V8 engine than its predecessor as well as the optional F1-inspired paddle-shift gearbox, but it was lighter – thanks to mostly aluminium construction – and even more refined.

A new flagship, front-engined V12 grand tourer, the 550 Maranello, blew away the lingering dust of the 1980s while stylistically nodding to the legacy of the iconic Daytona. In the year Schumacher claimed his final world title Ferrari launched the 612 Scaglietti, a four-seater whose name and style was a homage to the 1950s' 375MM, for which film director Roberto Rossellini commissioned a bespoke coupé body from Modenese coachbuilder Sergio Scaglietti.

BELOW: The 612 Scaglietti offered four seats as well as immense power within a retro-styled bodyshell.

On the track, the Schumacher era came to a close with a changing of the guard as rival teams rose to challenge Ferrari's dominance. A moment of madness during qualifying in Monaco, when Schumacher spun and blocked the track while Renault's Fernando Alonso was on a faster lap, prompted Ferrari president Luca di Montezemolo to muse that his superstar was reaching his sell-by date. Schumacher was duly nudged into retirement at the end of the season in favour of young Finn Kimi Räikkönen. Jean Todt moved aside in favour of sporting director Stefano Domenicali, and Ross Brawn announced that he would take a sabbatical to go trout fishing.

RIGHT: While the 248 F1 car was a return to form, Schumacher had a fight on his hands in 2006 in the form of newly crowned champion Fernando Alonso (following).

FIAT

WORLD DOMINATION

Ferrari

THE ROAD TO INDEPENDENCE

From the outside, the transition from one era to the next appeared seamless. Michael Schumacher retired from the Formula 1 frontline but energetically took up a new role as an ambassador and development driver for Ferrari's road-going cars.

Jean Todt moved "upstairs" as chief executive officer, handing the F1 team principal role to his chosen successor, Stefano Domenicali. Aldo Costa, Ross Brawn's understudy, became technical director of the F1 programme as Brawn embarked on a year's sabbatical. Costa's new car, the F2007, won from pole position first time out in the hands of Schumacher's replacement, Kimi Räikkönen.

Still, those schooled in Maranello politics caught a whiff of thwarted ambition in the air. Brawn, it was said, had wanted to be team principal – and, indeed, post-sabbatical, he returned in that role with the Honda F1 team. But the rumblings went deeper than that, and Ferrari were not the only team in which ambition was about to lead to folly.

OPPOSITE: In 2013 Ferrari launched the LaFerrari, bringing F1-derived hybrid engine technology to the road for the first time.

After two relatively quiet seasons by their standards, Ferrari were back near the top of their game in 2007 thanks to a technically advanced car and the end of the tyre war between rival suppliers Michelin and Bridgestone. The Japanese company won the right to exclusively supply the entire grid, a situation which played conveniently into Ferrari's hands since the Scuderia had been designing their cars around the characteristics of Bridgestone's tyres for the previous eight seasons. Michelin's departure caused Renault, which had delivered Fernando Alonso to the drivers' title in 2005 and 2006, to fall off the proverbial cliff.

BELOW: Kimi Räikkönen (centre) beat Fernando Alonso (right) to the world championship at the final round in 2007

ABOVE: The F2007 was among the most competitive cars of the 2007 season.

Having moved to McLaren, Alonso had a competitive car in which to fight Räikkönen and Felipe Massa for the world championship. But he also had to contend with a young upstart in the garage next door, one whose career had been supported by McLaren since he was a teenager: Lewis Hamilton. As a peculiar and increasingly rancorous dynamic evolved between Alonso and Hamilton, a four-way battle for the title developed between the McLaren and Ferrari drivers. In racing terms this was a vintage year.

Politically, too, it delivered in even more highly charged intrigue. The row, which became known as "Spygate", began in May with the discovery of white powder on the floor of the Ferrari garage in Monaco, and escalated from week to week as new revelations surfaced.

The powder was detergent, believed to have been added to the cars' fuel systems as sabotage by former chief mechanic

Nigel Stepney. A key figure in transforming Ferrari's occasionally slapdash trackside operations from 1997 onwards, Stepney supposedly coveted a more senior engineering role – perhaps even technical director – in the recent shake-up but had been parked in a factory job instead.

Subsequent revelations connected Stepney with McLaren chief designer Mike Coughlan, similarly frustrated by lack of opportunities to move onwards and upwards in his own organization. The whistleblower was a Woking copy shop employee who had been given a tranche of Ferrari technical documents, 780 pages no less, to duplicate by Coughlan's wife.

By September the slow drip of revelations had caused toxic levels of paranoia and suspicion to accumulate. Though it became apparent that Stepney and Coughlan planned to use their haul of Ferrari intellectual property to approach other

teams for senior technical positions, questions remained over who knew what, and how much, within McLaren. On September 13 – two days after a smiling Schumacher pulled the covers off the brand new F430 Scuderia at the Frankfurt motor show – racing's governing body handed McLaren a record $100 million dollar fine and deleted their constructors' championship points. Ferrari therefore ran unchallenged to the constructors' title, while Räikkönen claimed the drivers' crown with victory at the season-ending Brazilian Grand Prix.

A year later Brazil would host another thriller, albeit in different circumstances. The political temperature had subsided slightly as McLaren's new car passed a forensic technical investigation to determine if any Ferrari design DNA was present. Räikkönen's title defence got off to a bad start with an engine failure at the Australian Grand Prix, and he won

ABOVE: Ferrari replaced the 360 Modena with the F430, an even more potent junior supercar powered by an all-new V8 engine design.

just two races as team-mate Massa emerged as the most likely championship contender.

Massa's hopes hit a setback in the infamous Singapore Grand Prix in which Renault's Nelson Piquet Jr crashed deliberately to engineer a Safety Car period which benefitted his team-mate Fernando Alonso. When Massa, leading the race, came into the pits, his flustered team signalled him to go while the fuel hose was still attached to his car. The retirement proved costly and, three rounds later, Massa needed to win the final race of the season with Hamilton no higher than sixth to take the drivers' title.

On a gloomy and intermittently wet day Massa won from pole position and the celebrations began in the Ferrari garage as

BELOW: Failure to finish the 2008 Singapore Grand Prix after a pitlane miscue cost Felipe Massa dearly.

he crossed the line – only for Hamilton to make the vital pass for fifth place at the final corner of the last lap. From the top step of the podium, Massa tearfully acknowledged his home crowd in a poignant display of sportsmanship.

The development war between McLaren and Ferrari in the final months of 2008 exhausted both teams and distracted from the pressing matter of new rules to come the following season. Both teams entered a competitive slump in 2009 from which it took several seasons to recover.

Ferrari lost the guiding hand of Todt when he left to run for the presidency of the FIA. Massa also suffered an alarming accident in Hungary when a spring detached from the car in front and struck him on the head, fracturing his skull.

BELOW: Felipe Massa (centre) won the 2008 season-ending Brazilian Grand Prix from pole but lost the drivers' title by a single point.

FIAT

LEFT: The 2008 title fight drew resources from the design programme for the following year, and the 2009 F60 was disappointingly uncompetitive.

ABOVE: Fernando Alonso (left) quit in 2014 after a series of rows with new team principal Marco Mattiacci.

Old habits crept in as technical director Aldo Costa was scapegoated for the on-track failures. He moved on to Mercedes, becoming a key figure in that team's domination during the era to come. Signing Alonso as lead driver brought a certain level of intensity and the cars were good enough to win races if not quite championships, and three times Alonso was a frustrated runner-up.

The internal atmosphere soured as F1 transitioned to a new technical formula with turbocharged hybrid engines and Ferrari's solution wasn't good enough. Under pressure from Luca di Montezemolo to fire the head of the engine department, team principal Stefano Domenicali refused and resigned. His replacement, Marco Mattiacci, lasted eight months, during which time he fell out with Alonso, who was so desperate to leave that he went to McLaren, whence he had departed under a cloud seven years earlier.

Why all the sudden scrutiny and politics? Di Montezemolo himself was under considerable pressure, and not even his gilded track record could render him immune from the slump of 2014. This was because moves were afoot to demerge Ferrari from the parent company via a partial stock exchange flotation and it was a poor moment indeed to perform far below the expected level.

At the end of the year Di Montezemolo was shown the door and his place taken by his ultimate boss, Fiat Chrysler Automobiles chairman Sergio Marchionne. Born in Italy and raised in Canada, Marchionne conducted his business affairs with an iron fist which belied his nondescript appearance. Having attained degrees in philosophy, commerce and law as well as an MBA, Marchionne learned the inner workings of business as a tax specialist and chartered accountant at Deloitte & Touche before climbing through a series of executive posts in global companies which brought him to the eye of Fiat's controlling Agnelli family.

As Ferrari rose to self-sufficiency during the Schumacher years, its parent company's fortunes were on the slide, and when Marchionne was placed in overall charge of Fiat in 2004 it had lost $7 billion the previous year. He embarked on a radical – and often unpopular – programme of cost-cutting which turned around Fiat and enabled it to buy into the failing American car manufacturer Chrysler in 2009.

By 2014 the financial renaissance of both companies was complete and they were merged. The next stage of Marchionne's plan was to set Ferrari on a "separate path", listing 10 per cent of the company on the New York Stock Exchange, while allocating the remaining shares among the existing investors.

OVERLEAF:
Ferrari kept pace with the times by embracing downsized engines boosted by turbochargers. Launched in 2015, the 488 raised the bar in its class.

MICHELIN

OPPOSITE: Mattia Binotto moved from technical director to team principal in 2019.

BELOW: Opened in 2010, the Ferrari World Abu Dhabi theme park features the world's fastest rollercoaster.

The separation acknowledged that these companies were now two very different propositions, one a mass-market car maker which required further investment to carve out market share, the other a prestigious luxury brand as well as a builder of performance cars. Ferrari's prancing horse logo now adorns countless lines of merchandise; indeed, should you visit the Ferrari World Abu Dhabi theme park and, having ridden the Ferrari-themed fastest rollercoaster in the world, you can buy a toy camel emblazoned with the logo.

On the first day of trading in Ferrari shares in October 2015, Marchionne was invited to ring the famous NYSE bell to signify Wall Street had opened for business. Three months later, the Fiat Chrysler Group in effect sold the car manufacturer it had bought in 1969 by floating its 80 per cent share in Milan, though the Agnelli dynasty retained 24 per cent. Piero Ferrari continues to own 10 per cent of the company. Gianni Agnelli's grandson John Elkann took over as Ferrari chairman after Marchionne's untimely death in 2018.

On the track, Ferrari went from strength to strength. Under the technical leadership of the studious Mattia Binotto the F1

WEICHAI
潍柴
MAHLE
PIRELLI
UPS
M. BINOTTO

2015 FORMUL
RONAS
YSIA GRAND
MPUR
mula 1

team rebounded to become world championship challengers again, though they fell short despite recruiting four-times champion Sebastian Vettel. In the more mass-market fields of motor racing, Ferrari also scored hits, winning the GT class at Le Mans and expanding the Ferrari Challenge one-make series into new territories.

OPPOSITE: Sebastian Vettel led Ferrari to more race wins but fell short of clinching the world championship.

BELOW: The racing version of the 488 won its class in the Le Mans 24 Hours.

On the road, there is a class-leading Ferrari in virtually every segment of the sportscar market, the appropriately named 812 Superfast having recently supplanted the iconic V12-powered F12, the GTC4 Lusso providing space for four, and the Portofino and Roma offering in twin-turbocharged V8 form what the iconic California delivered in the 1960s.

The mid-engined V8 line has continued to evolve from the 360 Modena through the F430, 458 and 488 to the recently launched F8, Ferrari's most powerful V8-powered car ever thanks to the addition of twin turbochargers. As a pointer to a possible future, the SF90 Stradale augments four-litre twin-turbo V8 with three electric motors, yielding a combined power output of 986bhp.

All of these cars are built only at Maranello, where the window of Enzo Ferrari's old office still overlooks the factory gate.

BELOW: Ferrari's flagship car for the new decade is the SF90, the company's first plug-in hybrid – three electric motors and a turbocharged V8 output a combined 986bhp.

FERRARI IN POPULAR CULTURE

AN IMAGE TO DIE FOR

"The 1961 Ferrari 250GT California. Less than a hundred were made. My father spent three years restoring this car. It is his love. It is his passion..."
"...It is his fault he didn't lock the garage."

In the cult classic movie *Ferris Bueller's Day Off,* a popular teen fakes illness to avoid school for the day, joyrides in his friend's father's classic car – and all manner of absurdly improbable scrapes ensue. Come the final reel, the car needs another extensive restoration, though the vehicle which was subjected to the various on-screen indignities was actually a replica which attracted a trademark-infringement lawsuit from Ferrari.

Beneath the entertaining hokum there's an emotional layer to the storytelling in which the car acts as a cypher for the unseen father who loves a valuable object more than his son. And yet the car is also a prisoner, after a fashion: cherished, buffed, kept in an air-conditioned glass box, but rarely used for the purpose for which it was intended.

OPPOSITE: Welcome to the 1980s – the Testarossa perfectly matched the sharp styling of the protagonists in TV's *Miami Vice*.

BELOW: Adolfo Celi (left) played a character clearly inspired by Enzo Ferrari (right) in the movie *Grand Prix*, though Enzo claimed he couldn't see the resemblance.

Such has been the fate of many old and rare Ferraris in recent decades as turbulent global stock markets drive demand for alternative investments. The movie's original script called for a Mercedes, but during pre-production director John Hughes had a moment of clarity: the father is described as loving his classic car "more than life itself". It had to be selected just as carefully as the human members of the cast.

Enzo Ferrari well knew the importance of perception to his marque's mythology, and he cultivated the image of the shadowy figure manipulating events from afar, eyes always

concealed behind dark glasses. In 1966, Hollywood shadowed the Formula 1 circus as John Frankenheimer shot *Grand Prix* in and around the various race events. The Italian actor Adolfo Celi, best known to international audiences as James Bond's nemesis Largo in *Thunderball* played Agostini Manetta, a slippery and Machiavellian team owner clearly modelled on Enzo – who affected a lack of interest in the entire affair and reckoned he couldn't see any likeness, though by all accounts he was quietly delighted when he was shown the rushes.

ABOVE: The 250GT California once owned by James Coburn was the first car to sell for over $10 million.

Cars such as the California were built specifically to appeal to the West Coast market of wealthy socialites and movie stars, for whom European sophistication and exoticism trumped the pure muscle offered by US rivals. James Coburn was talked into buying one by Steve McQueen while in Europe filming *The Great Escape* and, in May 2008, that same car became the first to change hands for more than $10 million.

In the 1980s, Ferrari's appeal crossed over into the mainstream, perfectly appealing to a new, badge-conscious, upwardly mobile generation for whom conspicuous

consumption defined the dream. In some countries during the 1970s, particularly Italy, driving an ostentatiously expensive car had been an open invitation to be kidnapped, and Ferrari's flagship models embodied a suitable level of styling restraint.

Economic growth in the new decade prompted a huge cultural shift. While the likes of the staid, square-rigged 400i remained the province of what one might call the moneyed old European demographic – the cashmere-sweater-over-the-shoulders crowd – more dynamic models such as the Testarossa and 308GTB offered the perfect wealth-flaunting platform for those making a mint in the city.

Underlining this thrusting decade's confidence that everything was attainable, posters of Ferrari models became as *de rigueur* as black ash furniture in teenagers' bedrooms and lit up the screen in popular TV shows. In *Magnum P.I.*, the titular private detective, for all that he seemed permanently on the verge of eviction by his landlord and performed little in the way of paid work, motored around Hawaii in a red 308GTS. Just two owners later, one of the cars used in filming sold for $181,500 at auction in 2018.

But the 308 was already rather long in the tooth as the 1980s got into gear. It was the Testarossa which really rode the consumerist wave and became – literally – Ferrari's poster child. Launched in 1984 it was initially treated with disdain by traditionalists, who felt the swooping waistline and exaggerated strakes on each side flirted with vulgarity. The latter features – necessary because US regulations prohibited an open cooling aperture for the mid-mounted flat-12 engine – became iconic, propelled into the cultural stratosphere by its presence on zeitgeisty crime drama *Miami Vice*,

With its fashionably loud iconography, edgy setting and subject matter (undercover cops masquerading as high-rolling drug dealers) and propulsive, angular electronic soundtrack,

OPPOSITE: Actor Tom Selleck played the titular character in the iconic 1980s TV series *Magnum P.I.*, roaring around Hawaii in a red 308GTS.

OPPOSITE: A Ferrari 641 F1 car is among the exhibits in the New York Museum of Modern Art.

BELOW: The Testarossa became an icon of the 1980s. Posters of it adorned bedroom walls worldwide and Ferrari could barely make enough to fulfil demand.

Miami Vice epitomised an era of style over substance. Co-protagonist James "Sonny" Crockett, played by Don Johnson, drove an open-top 365 GTB/4 in the show's first two seasons, though the vehicles used in filming were actually fibreglass replicas based on Chevrolet Corvette chassis. As the show percolated worldwide the inevitable cease-and-desist order came from Maranello, albeit laced with a remarkable offer: use of genuine Ferraris in the form of two Testarossas. For a company generally not given to providing cars for filming this was truly remarkable; it's said that Enzo was a fan of the show.

Other celebrity owners of the time included Elton John, Rod Stewart, Michael Jordan, OJ Simpson and Mike Tyson. Slightly less celebrated were the drug dealers and city spivs who also found the Testarossa's look-at-me presence irresistible, including the notorious penny-stock scammer Jordan Belfort, who was memorably brought to life by Leonardo di Caprio in Martin Scorsese's *The Wolf of Wall Street*.

GOODYEAR
1
GOODYEAR
GOODYEAR

OPPOSITE: Notorious for destroying three classic Ferraris and reporting them stolen to claim the insurance money, Lord Brocket exploited his profile to carve out a career on reality TV.

Not that such characters would have been entertained at Maranello: before the boom turned to bust, demand far outstripped supply and many new Testarossa owners sold their cars straight away to queue-jumpers for a healthy cash mark-up. This being the 1980s, plenty of them had acquired the cars specifically for that purpose. Even after the economic winds turned chilly, the Testarossa retained a certain cachet within particular fraternities: in 1993 one of the kidnappers of Kevyn Wynn, daughter of Las Vegas strip casino magnate Steve Wynn, was caught when he used his share of the ransom cash to buy a second-hand 512TR – in white, naturally.

The history of pre-owned Ferraris continues to capture the popular imagination, whether their previous guardians are celebrities or crooks – or both. Charles Nall-Cain inherited a peerage, the title Lord Brocket, and the family's Hertfordshire mansion at the age of 15, when his grandfather died in 1967. As with many relics of aristocracy at the time, the 25-bedroom property and its 1400-acre grounds were subsiding into disrepair. With the aid of loans, Lord Brocket converted it into a luxury hotel and conference centre with a pair of golf courses.

Business boomed during the 1980s and, with the aid of further leverage on the mansion, Lord Brocket began to amass a collection of Italian classics. Soaring interest rates as the economy slammed into reverse gear left him struggling to repay the debts – while the value of his car collection headed south.

Under cover of night in May 1991, Lord Brocket and three employees dismantled four of the most precious cars in the collection – three of them Ferraris – cutting up the bodywork with angle grinders and melting the pieces in a furnace. The dismantled chassis and other components were hidden in various other properties and various items are believed to have been buried – never to be found. Brocket's insurers refused to pay up and he was subsequently arrested and charged with

LORD
LORD BROCKET

fraud, to which an obtaining money by deception charge was added when it emerged he had sold Microsoft CEO Jon Shirley a fake 250 GT SWB Berlinetta which had been built from a lesser car and given a bogus chassis number.

OPPOSITE: Demi Moore drove a Ferrari Enzo in the movie *Charlie's Angels*.

One of the Ferraris, a 1951 340 America originally carrying coach-built bodywork by Vignale, was rebuilt after the chassis and engine were recovered. Initially auctioned at $600,000, it has since changed hands several times for increasing values and is now believed to be in Japan. After serving two years of a five-year sentence he was released and parlayed his notoriety into an appearance on the reality TV show *I'm A Celebrity... Get Me Out Of Here!*

The behaviour of celebrity Ferrari owners continues to vex and exercise the guardians of the brand, and the company's press offices worldwide are notoriously choosy regarding whom they lend cars to, particularly musicians and influencers who are wont to court publicity. Rapper A$AP Twelvyy appeared to set an elderly 348 on fire after performing stunts in it during the video for the song "Hop Out". The sheer desirability of the brand is irresistible to those who inhabit the overlapping worlds of reality television and influencer culture, such as *90 Day Fiancé* star Brittany Banks, for instance, whose videos blend rap, highly sexualised dancing, gratuitous product placement, and the occasional wander around luxury car showrooms.

In the 21st century, celebrity carries a potent marketing value, and many individuals with a large social media following shamelessly exploit their appeal to the aspirational youth demographic. In 2019 Ferrari decided enough was enough and, in effect, declared war on influencers. After German fashion designer Philipp Plein posted a number of pictures on his Instagram account of bikini-clad women gyrating atop his 812 Superfast while washing it, along with other images of his own products on the car, he received a stiff takedown order: "This

behaviour tarnishes the reputation of Ferrari's brands," said the letter.

After much public rancour between the two parties the issue was finally resolved in a Genovese court – in Ferrari's favour. It was a landmark ruling which sent a chill through the influencer community. The court upheld Ferrari's claim of trademark infringement, denigration and discredit, as well as unlawful commercial use of the Ferrari logo. Plein's counter-argument, that he was simply sharing elements of his private life and that the images served no commercial purpose, was dismissed. "The Ferrari trademark evokes in the public the characteristics of exclusivity and absence of vulgarity, which are incompatible with the car wash images/videos," was the rather prim summing-up, one which has ramifications for all who seek to piggy-back product placement on others' brands for their own gain.

Thirty-five years after the makers of *Ferris Bueller's Day Off* had their collars felt by Ferrari's trademark police, the message rang loudly once more, like the Modena church bells: "Don't mess with the badge."

LEFT: The 250GT California seen in *Ferris Bueller's Day Off* was actually a replica based on Chevrolet mechanicals. Ferrari sued on the grounds of trademark infringement.

INDEX

Numbers in italics are the pages on which a caption appears.

CREDITS

The publishers would like to thank the following sources for their kind permission to reproduce the pictures in this book.

ALAMY: /Photo 12: 142; /Realy Easy Star/Giuseppe Masci: 149; /Reuters: 145; /Shawshots: 11; /United Archives GmbH: 154-155

GETTY IMAGES: /Barrett-Jackson: 124-125; /Mel Bouzad: 152; /CBS Photo Archive: 146; /Bernard Cahier: 144; /David Cooper/Toronto Star: 115; / Martyn Lucy: 138-139; /Marka/Universal Images Group: 23; /National Motor Museum/Heritage Images: 50-51, 88-89, 114; /Alessia Pierdomenico/ Bloomberg: 4, 120; /Emilio Ronchini/Mondadori: 39; /Sjo: 94-95

MOTORSPORT IMAGES: 58, 62, 73, 106; /Jeff Bloxham/LAT: 66-67; / Ercole Colombo/Studio Colombo: 68, 69, 78, 90; /Steve Etherington/LAT: 102, 108, 116-117; /JEP: 137; /LAT: 12, 13, 14, 15, 16, 22, 24-25, 26-27, 28, 29, 30-31, 32, 33, 34-35, 37, 44, 47, 48-49, 56-57, 59, 65, 70, 72, 76-77, 79, 91, 92-93, 97, 111; /David Phipps: 36, 53, 54; /Rainer Schlegelmilch: 42, 45, 64, 71, 87, 100, 104-105, 110, 123, 126, 128-129; /Sutton Images: 82, 85, 86, 103, 107, 112-113, 122, 127, 136; /Mark Sutton: 135; /Steven Tee: 130

PA IMAGES: /Fabio Fiorani/IPA MilestoneMedia: 8

SHUTTERSTOCK: /Anglia Press Agency Ltd: 148; /Burachet: 134; /ermess: 74-75; /Cameron Laird: 151; /Time & Life Pictures: 20; /yousang: 132-133

WIKIMEDIA COMMONS: /GTHO: 46

Every effort has been made to acknowledge correctly and contact the source and/or copyright holder of each picture any unintentional errors or omissions will be corrected in future editions of this book.